Food & Drink Logos

A handbook of food & drink
marks of identity, compiled
& edited by Counter-Print.

With special thanks to all
the contributors for their
support, time and talent.

ISBN 978-1-915392-02-2

| **Green Door Pizza** | Hospitality | 2021 | Kevin Rosales kevinrosales.com |

| **Neptunes Pizzeria** | Takeaway pizza business | 2021 | Ben Galbraith Design bengalbraith.co.nz |

DOG EAT DOGS
HOT DOGS
ホットドッグ

QUEENSTOWN
NEW ZEALAND

@DOG_EAT_DOGS

Banger

Gourmet hot dogs, burgers & fries

2021

Angel & Anchor
angelandanchor.com

Sup Dog

Open late food spot offering brats, dogs & sausages

2019

Lazaris
wearelazaris.com

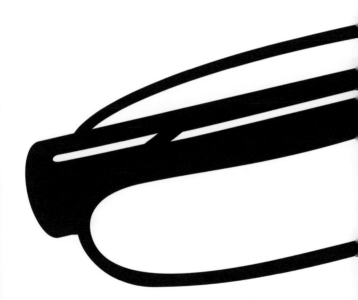

Brandon Nickerson
bnicks.com

Burger King Quick service 2021 Jones Knowles
restaurant Ritchie
jkrglobal.com

The Empanada Kitchen

Empanadas & sauces

2014

makebardo
makebardo.com

Baba Kebab

Grab & go doner restaurant

2018

Lina Bassiouny
linabassiouny.com

| **Moody's** | Ice cream | 2020 | Abby Haddican Studio abbyhaddican.com |

| **Suomen Jäätelö** | Ice cream factory | 2016 | Werklig werklig.com |

Jefferson's   Ice cream   2019   Everything
In Between
e-i-b.com

Sorbet for Jam3   Internal platform   2020   Asís
that allows   weareasis.co
Jam3 to quickly
access their
freelancer roster

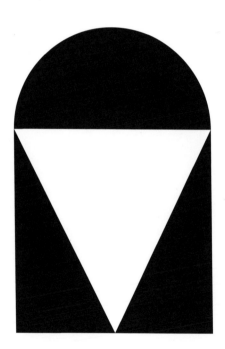

**Conze at
The Spot**

Fried food
served in tasty
waffle cones

2021

Type08
type08.com

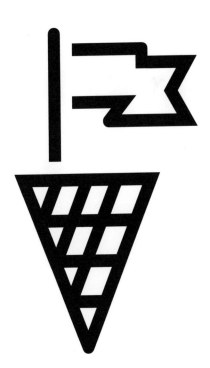

Small Talk
Coffee & Snacks

Bagel & baked
goods store

2020

After Hours
afterhoursstudio.
com.au

Happy Maple   Vegan doughnuts   2016   Studio Garbett
                                                                    garbett.com.au

HAPPY MAPLE

Cinnzeo   Canadian-style   2020   Daughter
                bakeries   daughtercreative.
                                                                 com

The Loaf   Independent,   2020   Alt Design
                 family-owned   alt-design.net
                 artisan bakery

Swell Bakery   Bakery   2022   Jay Fletcher
                                         jfletcherdesign.com

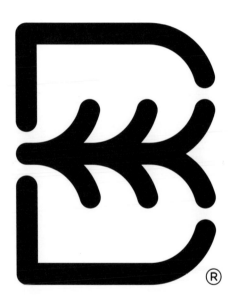

Breadwinners Fresh bread   2016   Bread Collective
                   delivery service   breadcollective.co.uk

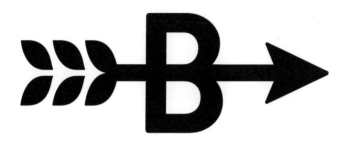

Special Food   Therapeutic   2013   Mubien Brands
Service   diet solutions   mubien.com

 SPECIAL
FOOD
SERVICE

**West Coast
Grocery Co**

Beer &
restaurant

2018

Sally Morrow
Creative
sallymorrowcreative.
com

Jästbolaget AB   Yeast   2015   SuperTuesday /
                       manufacturer   Rob Clarke
                                                         supertuesday.se /
                                                         robclarke.com

**New Hokkaido
Beverage Co**

Beer & hard
seltzers

2019

Sally Morrow
Creative
sallymorrowcreative.
com

Senn Bierwerks   Craft brewery   2016   Carpenter Collective
carpentercollective.
com

| **Boulevard Brewing Co** | Brewery & bar | 2018 | Carpenter Collective carpentercollective.com |

| **Greater Good** | Craft beer & games bar | 2016 | Doublenaut doublenaut.com |

Carrot Waste management software   2021   Heydays / Goods heydays.no / goods.no

Carrot

Vivo Live Food Healthy food restaurant   2019   invade design invade.design

Dotte Mobile Grocer

Mobile grocery store

2019

Carpenter Collective carpentercollective.com

Regalo Orchard   Orchard &
event venue

2020

Carpenter Collective
carpentercollective.
com

The Brass Onion   Low country
restaurant & bar   2018   Carpenter Collective
carpentercollective.
com

PLATES + POURS

Lá Lành

Sustainably
produced
vegetables

2020

Rice
thisisrice.com

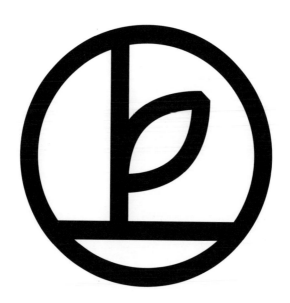

Always Fruit

Telecommunications equipment distributor

2016

Mubien Brands
mubien.com

Grono

Restaurant
& apartments

2019

Marta Gawin Studio
martagawin.com

Bindella
Restaurant
Tel Aviv

Italian restaurant   2014

Studio Koniak
koniakdesign.com

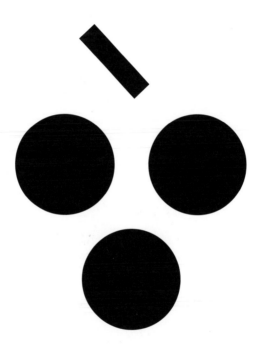

BARRELS & BEYOND

Organic corporate 2009
fruit baskets

Jost Brands
jost.co

County Supplies

London-based
fruit & vegetable
wholesaler

2019

Jost Brands
jost.co

Shinone Apple Farm	Apple farm	2018	Commune commune-inc.jp

Nude na Ongaku	Music program on UHB (Hokkaido Cultural Broadcasting)	2016	Commune commune-inc.jp

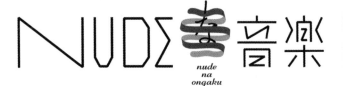

**Happy Food
by Petra**

Vegan food
author, journalist
& chef

2018

Add Studio
addstudio.se

Noji Produce   Produce
distributor   2020   Brandon Nickerson
bnicks.com

| **güüd** | Fruit juice | 2019 | VRLN |
| | | | vrln.studio |

Limón	Fast food	2020	Heydays /
	restaurant		Goods
			heydays.no /
			goods.no

Nilus	NPO for food waste reduction	2018	Asís weareasis.co

Cafetoria	Organic coffee roaster	2018	Diferente diferente.info

ORGANIC COFFEE

CAFETORIA

ROASTED WHOLEHEARTEDLY

Coffee Kind   Coffee   2012   Jay Fletcher
                    subscription   jfletcherdesign.com
                    company

COFFEE KIND

| **Kelly Deli** | Asian food | 2018 | Without |
| | | | without.studio |

| **Gyoza Bar** | Dining bar | 2015 | Commune |
| | | | commune-inc.jp |

**Black Sea
Food Festival**
Food festival near
the Black Sea
2018

VRLN
vrln.studio

**Broadway
Restaurant**
Restaurant
2019

Toma Studio
tomastudio.eu

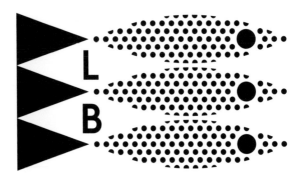

**The Coop
Rotisserie
and Larder**

Homestyle
food & larder

2021

Studio Garbett
garbett.com.au

**The Coop
Rotisserie
and Larder**

Homestyle
food & larder

2021

Studio Garbett
garbett.com.au

Poogan's Southern Kitchen   Restaurant   2020   Jay Fletcher
jfletcherdesign.com

Gallitas   Homemade chicken wings   2021   Diferente
diferente.info

**Mr.Chicken
& Co.**

Chicken-based
fast food delivery

2021

Type08
type08.com

**Poogan's
Southern
Kitchen**
Restaurant
2020
Jay Fletcher
jfletcherdesign.com

**Poogan's
Smokehouse**

Restaurant

2015

Jay Fletcher
jfletcherdesign.com

77

Pandeli Foods   Indian food
                   & drink   2017   Rob Clarke
                                                        robclarke.com

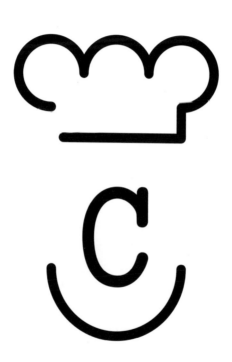

Zero Foodprint

A nonprofit organisation mobilising the food world around agricultural climate solutions

2014

Ryan Bosse Design
ryanbosse.com

**Hopewell
& Grace**

Restaurant

2013

Rob Clarke
robclarke.com

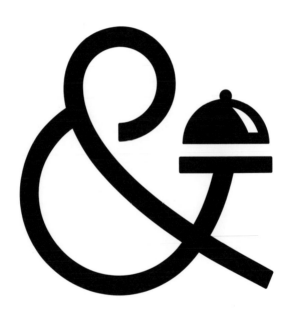

MORTON

&

PEPLOW

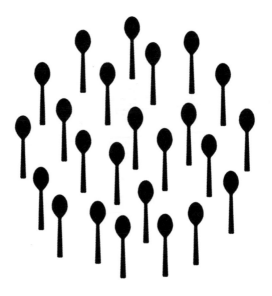

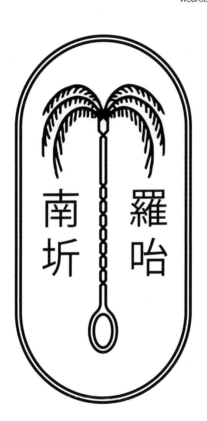

**Brancato's
Catering**

Catering

2019

Carpenter Collective
carpentercollective.
com

American Palate

Food book publisher

2012

Jay Fletcher
jfletcherdesign.com

Gourmet Factory

Catering service

2016

Asís
weareasis.co

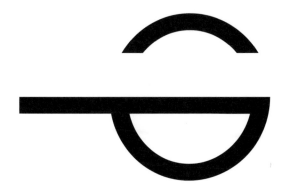

**Poogan's
Southern
Kitchen**

Restaurant

2020

Jay Fletcher
jfletcherdesign.com

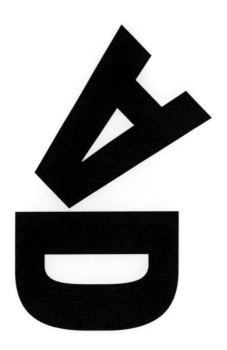

Acanteen Restaurant 2017 IWANT
iwantdesign.com

A
CANTEEN

Potter & Reid Hospitality/café 2022 Kevin Rosales
kevinrosales.com

Juice Traders   Online wine store   2020   After Hours
afterhoursstudio.
com.au

Sorbo Tequila   Handcrafted   2019   Lazaris
tequila   wearelazaris.com

Barrel One   Coffee roaster   2020   After Hours
                    & café   afterhoursstudio.
                                                       com.au

Dalston's Soda Company
Better for you sodas
2018
B&B Studio
bandb-studio.co.uk

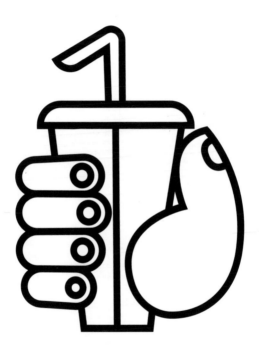

**Acid House
Coffee Shop**

Coffee shop
& store

2021

Folch /
Illustration
by Josep Puy
folchstudio.com

COFFEE SHOP

On the Way

Japanese
tea brand from
HAPPY TREE

2014

Commune
commune-inc.jp

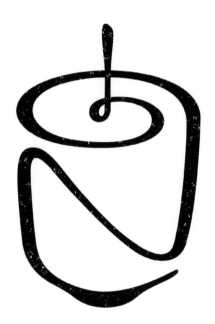

Intermezzo
Coffee
& Cocktails

Specialty coffee
shop & craft
cocktail bar

2019

Break Maiden
breakmaiden.co

Design by Twist /
Illustration by
Steve Gavan
designbytwist.com

Everleaf

Non-alcoholic
aperitifs

2019

Magpie Studio
magpie-studio.com

Index of Companies

Food & Drink Logos

Compiled and edited
by Counter-Print
counter-print.co.uk

Designed by Jon Dowling
& Céline Leterme

First Published in 2022
Reprinted in 2023

Copyright © Counter-Print

ISBN 978-1-915392-02-2

Printed in China